MathSmart

Multiplication & Division Games

Grade 3

This book belongs to:

Don

CONTENTS — Multiplication & Division Games • Grade Three

Cindy Caterpillar eats the leaves following the 2 times table and Calvin Caterpillar follows the 3 times table. Colour their paths in different colours. List the numbers that both Cindy and Calvin get through.

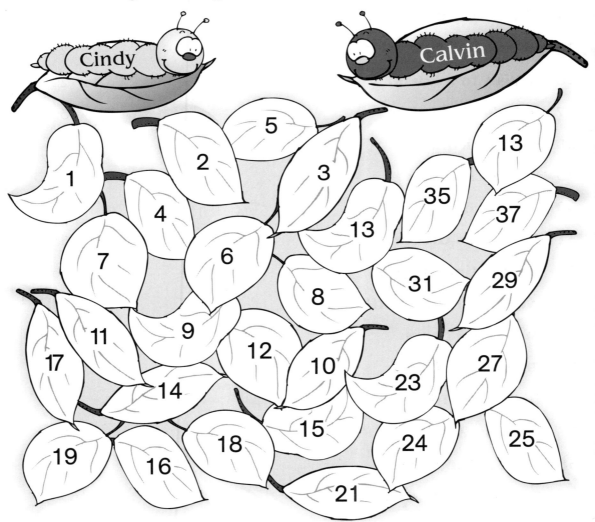

Both Cindy and Calvin get through numbers

_____ .

A Summer Game

Colour the numbers in the field following the 4 times table. Then complete what the children say with the representing letters in the coloured parts following the order of the numbers from least to greatest.

We need a ___ ___ ___ ___ ___

and a ___ ___ ___ to play this

game.

Help Ted paint the fences. Follow the 5 times table to colour the balusters yellow. Then colour the rest orange.

4 Gold Coins

Colour the coins following the 6 times table. Help Mr. Kennedy identify the gold coins from the fake ones.

Let's Go Camping

Follow the 7 times table and colour the path. Help the children get to the campsite.

7

14

21

28

27

35

42

41

48

49

56

54

63

About Michelle

Rearrange the numbers in each group following the 8 times table. Then write the letters on the books to solve the riddles.

What does Michelle like best?

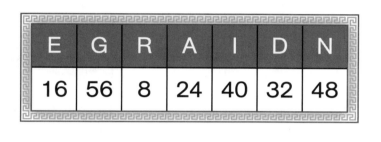

E	G	R	A	I	D	N
16	56	8	24	40	32	48

①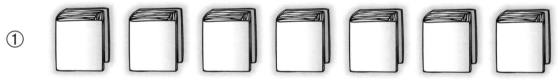

Where does Michelle like to go?

B	R	L	Y	A	I	R
40	64	24	72	56	32	48

②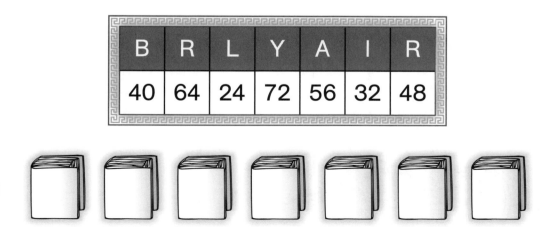

The Tempting Bananas

Follow the 9 times table and colour the path. Help Monkey Maurice get the bananas.

	98	100	109	
90	95	98	
72	85	89	90
63	79	85	81
89	72	72	71	72	80	89
80	65	63	62	63	71	81
71	59	53	45	54	62	72
	44	36	46
	36	27	35
	18	26
	9	17

Yummy Muffins

Draw muffins on each plate according to the multiplication sentences. Then fill in the blanks with the correct numbers.

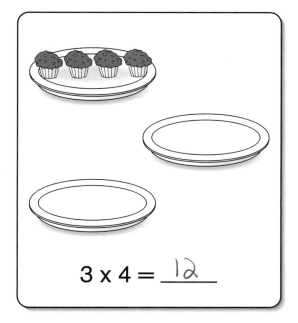

3 x 4 = __12__

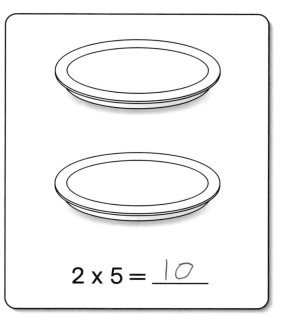

2 x 5 = __10__

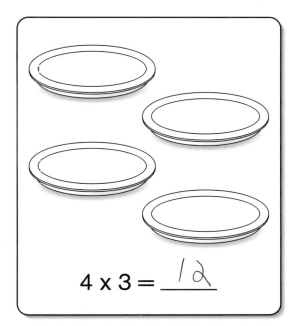

4 x 3 = __12__

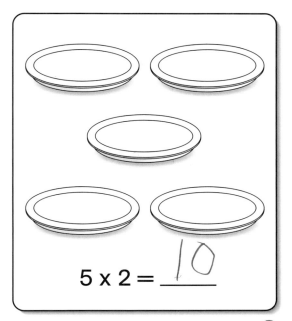

5 x 2 = __10__

Michelle's Markers

Draw lines to join the multiplication sentences with the same product. Help Michelle match the pens and the caps.

① 4 x 3
12

② 4 x 5
20

③ 6 x 3
18

④ 3 x 8
24

⑤ 9 x 1
9

A 5 x 4
20

B 6 x 4
24

C 2 x 6
12

D 3 x 3
9

E 2 x 9
18

Puzzle Time

Multiply and colour the matching pieces the same colour.

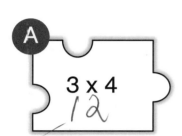

A

3 x 4

12

B

6 x 4

24

C

6 x 6

36

D

3 x 6

18

E

4 x 9

36

F

8 x 3

24

G

9 x 1

9

H

2 x 6

12

I

2 x 9

18

J

3 x 3

9

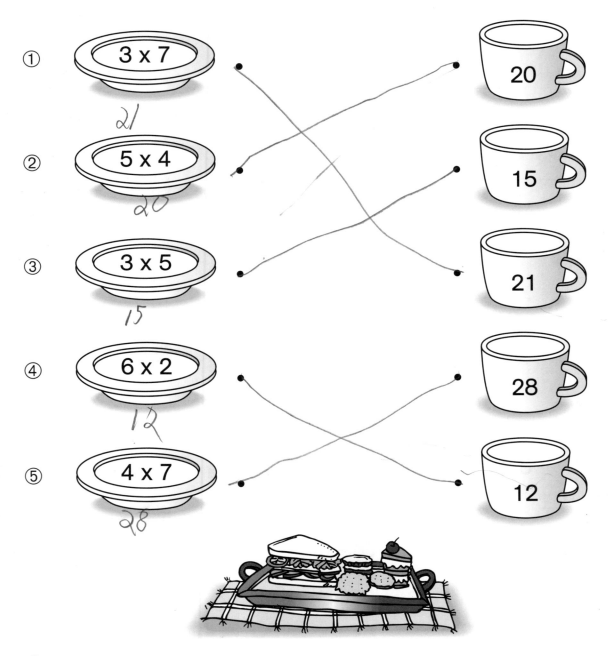

It's Tea Time

11

Match the cups with the saucers. Help Mom prepare the afternoon tea.

① 3 x 7
21

② 5 x 4
20

③ 3 x 5
15

④ 6 x 2
12

⑤ 4 x 7
28

20

15

21

28

12

12 Off to the Beach

Multiply. Colour the path with products between 10 and 25. Help Michelle and Ted get to the beach.

3 x 6 _18_

5 x 4 = 20

7 x 5 _35_

2 x 4 _8_

6 x 7 _42_

8 x 2 _16_

4 x 3 _12_

4 x 8 _32_

9 x 2 _18_

3 x 8 _24_

5 x 4 _20_

4 x 7 _28_

9 x 3 _27_

2 x 6 _12_

4 x 4 _16_

3 x 5 _15_

Boys and Toys

Match the multiplication sentences on the toys with the products on the boys' T-shirts. Write the representing letters on their boxes.

A: 4 x 3

B: 3 x 8

C: 2 x 9

D: 6 x 2

NUMBER GAME

E: 6 x 4

F: 3 x 6

G: 6 x 3

H: 4 x 6

I: 2 x 6

①

②

③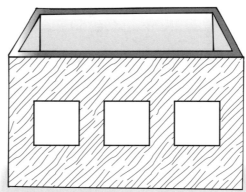

Cotton Candies

Cotton candies of different flavours were sold at Uncle Tom's food stall. Multiply. Then colour the cotton candy with the largest product pink and the one with the smallest product yellow.

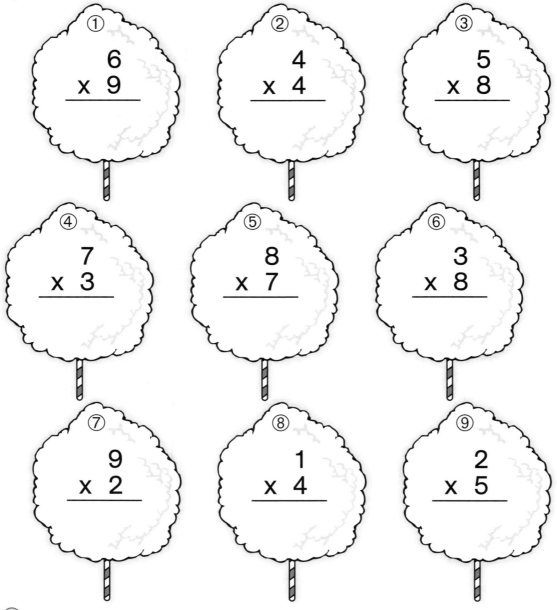

①
$$
\begin{array}{r}
6 \\
\times\ 9 \\
\hline
\end{array}
$$

②
$$
\begin{array}{r}
4 \\
\times\ 4 \\
\hline
\end{array}
$$

③
$$
\begin{array}{r}
5 \\
\times\ 8 \\
\hline
\end{array}
$$

④
$$
\begin{array}{r}
7 \\
\times\ 3 \\
\hline
\end{array}
$$

⑤
$$
\begin{array}{r}
8 \\
\times\ 7 \\
\hline
\end{array}
$$

⑥
$$
\begin{array}{r}
3 \\
\times\ 8 \\
\hline
\end{array}
$$

⑦
$$
\begin{array}{r}
9 \\
\times\ 2 \\
\hline
\end{array}
$$

⑧
$$
\begin{array}{r}
1 \\
\times\ 4 \\
\hline
\end{array}
$$

⑨
$$
\begin{array}{r}
2 \\
\times\ 5 \\
\hline
\end{array}
$$

Stocked up for Winter

Multiply. Then colour the path with increasing products to help Samuel Squirrel collect the acorns.

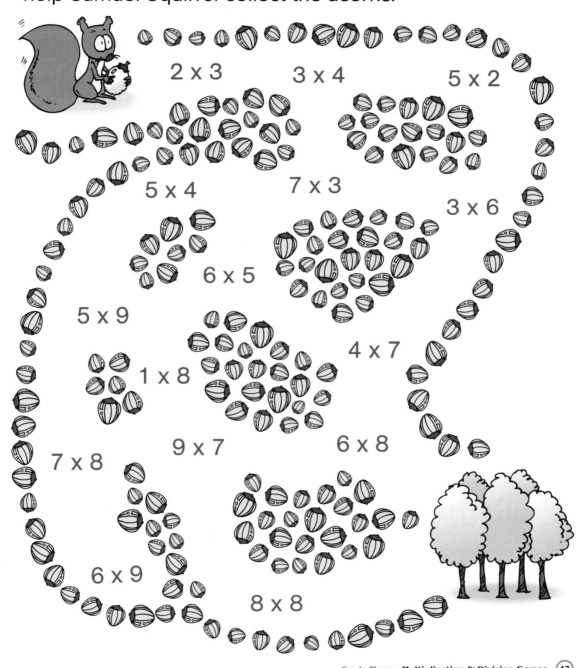

2 x 3 3 x 4 5 x 2

5 x 4 7 x 3 3 x 6

6 x 5

5 x 9 4 x 7

1 x 8

7 x 8 9 x 7 6 x 8

6 x 9 8 x 8

Colourful Beads

Multiply and match to see how many beads in each colour Michelle has. Write the colours on the bottles.

20 – red	16 – blue	45 – green
30 – yellow	36 – violet	48 – pink
21 – orange	63 – white	12 – black

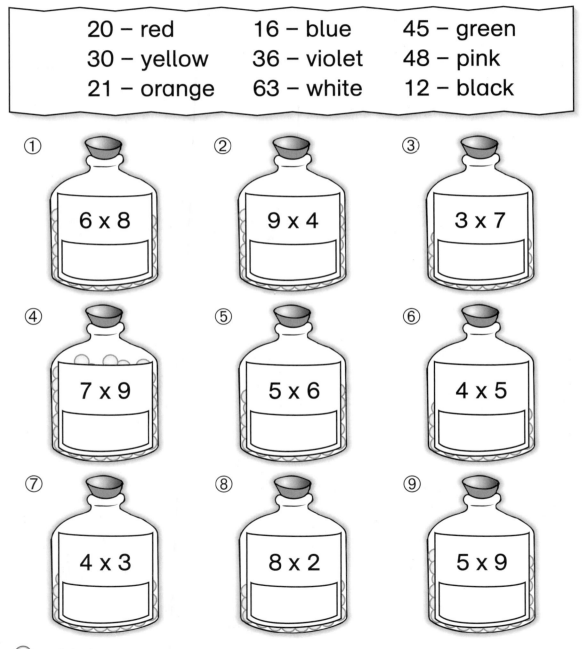

① 6 x 8

② 9 x 4

③ 3 x 7

④ 7 x 9

⑤ 5 x 6

⑥ 4 x 5

⑦ 4 x 3

⑧ 8 x 2

⑨ 5 x 9

Multiply. Then write the letters to find out where Michelle will go for vacation.

①   5 x 4 = _____   h

②   7 x 2 = _____   e

③   6 x 6 = _____   v

④   3 x 9 = _____   W

⑤   4 x 8 = _____   s

⑥   8 x 1 = _____   l

⑦   7 x 3 = _____   i

⑧   2 x 5 = _____   t

⑨   9 x 6 = _____   r

⑩   I'll go to ___ ___ ___ ___ ___ ___ ___ ___ .
                27   20   21   32   10   8   14   54

The Zoo

The children are visiting the zoo. Look at the picture and do the multiplication. Help the children find the answers.

① 3 elephants have _____ legs.   3 x ☐ = ☐

② 6 monkeys have _____ arms.   6 x ☐ = ☐

③ 8 flowers have _____ petals.   ☐ x ☐ = ☐

④ 5 rabbits have _____ tails.   ☐ x ☐ = ☐

⑤ 5 rabbits have _____ ears.   ☐ x ☐ = ☐

⑥ 3 elephants have_____ tusks.   ☐ x ☐ = ☐

Draw lines to connect the multiplication sentences to the answers. Use the letter on the same line with each number to help solve the riddle.

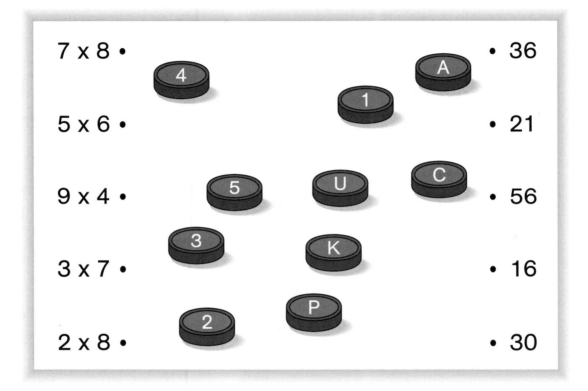

7 x 8 •

5 x 6 •

9 x 4 •

3 x 7 •

2 x 8 •

• 36

• 21

• 56

• 16

• 30

4 · A · 1 · 5 · U · C · 3 · K · 2 · P

What has no legs but can move across ice?

1	2	3	4	5

Ted's Toy Cars

Ted wants to divide his toy cars equally into groups. Help him circle the cars and write the number of groups in the boxes.

2 are in each group.

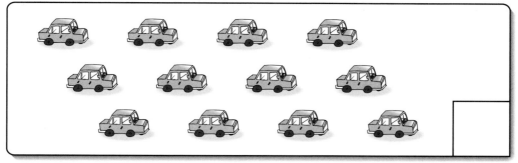

3 are in each group.

4 are in each group.

Collecting Seashells

6 children are sharing the seashells they have collected at the beach. Complete the division sentence to find how many seashells each child has.

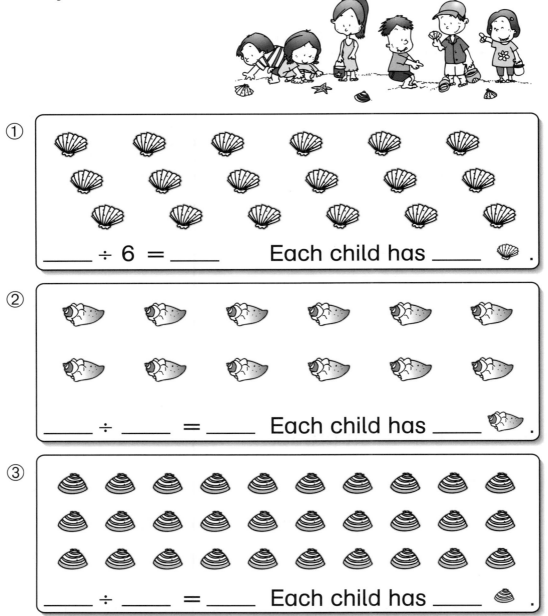

① _____ ÷ 6 = _____   Each child has _____ .

② _____ ÷ _____ = _____   Each child has _____ .

③ _____ ÷ _____ = _____   Each child has _____ .

1 Hungry Caterpillars

Cindy | Calvin | Both

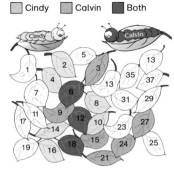

6, 12, and 18

2 A Summer Game

glove ; bat

3 A Painting Job

yellow | orange

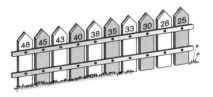

4 Gold Coins

Gold coins are: 6 ; 12 ; 18 ; 24 ; 30 ; 36 ; 42 ; 48 ; 54

5 Let's Go Camping

6 About Michelle

1. READING   2. LIBRARY

7 The Tempting Bananas

8 Yummy Muffins

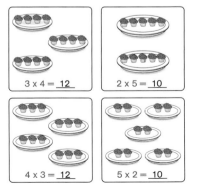

$3 \times 4 = \underline{12}$ $2 \times 5 = \underline{10}$

$4 \times 3 = \underline{12}$ $5 \times 2 = \underline{10}$

ANSWERS

9 Michelle's Markers

1. C   2. A   3. E
4. B   5. D

10 Puzzle Time

A – H   B – F   C – E
D – I   G – J

11 It's Tea Time

1. 21   2. 20   3. 15
4. 12   5. 28

12 Off to the Beach

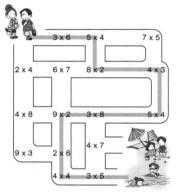

13 Boys and Toys

1. A ; D ; I   2. B ; E ; H   3. C ; F ; G

14 Cotton Candies

1. 54   2. 16   3. 40
4. 21   5. 56 – pink 6. 24
7. 18   8. 4 – yellow 9. 10

15 Stocked up for Winter

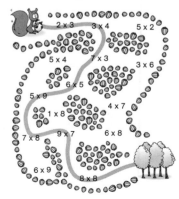

16 Colourful Beads

1. pink   2. violet   3. orange
4. white   5. yellow   6. red
7. black   8. blue   9. green

17 A Skiing Vacation

1. 20   2. 14   3. 36
4. 27   5. 32   6. 8
7. 21   8. 10   9. 54
10. Whistler

18 The Zoo

1. 12 ; 4 ; 12   2. 12 ; 2 ; 12
3. 40 ; 8 ; 5 ; 40   4. 5 ; 5 ; 1 ; 5
5. 10 ; 5 ; 2 ; 10   6. 6 ; 3 ; 2 ; 6

19 A Game on Ice

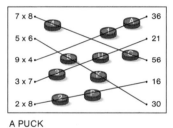

A PUCK

20 Ted's Toy Cars

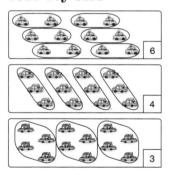

21 Collecting Seashells

1. 18 ; 3 ; 3   2. 12 ; 6 ; 2 ; 2
3. 30 ; 6 ; 5 ; 5

22 Food for Betty

Food with an answer of 6:

54 ÷ 9   36 ÷ 6   18 ÷ 3   42 ÷ 7   48 ÷ 8

23 What Are Their Names?

1. Algo   2. Happy   3. Spot
4. Doug   5. Jo Jo

24 The Carnival

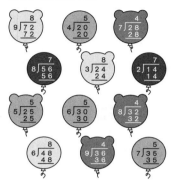

25 Hens and Eggs

1. green   2. blue   3. yellow
4. yellow   5. green   6. yellow
7. blue   8. blue   9. green
10. blue   11. yellow   12. green

26 A Visit to a Friend

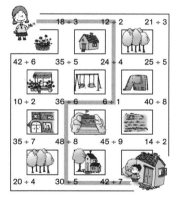

27 What's That?

1. 9   2. 5   3. 2
4. 7   5. 4   6. 1
7. 8   8. 3   9. 6
10. gorilla

28 Happy Birthday

1. 3   2. 4   3. 6
4. 8   5. 1   6. 7
7. 5   8. 9   9. 8
10. eight

29 In the Circus

1. 5 ; 15 ; 3 ; 5   2. 2 ; 4 ; 2 ; 2
3. 2 ; 12 ; 6 ; 2   4. 1 ; 6 ; 6 ; 1
5. 5 ; 10 ; 2 ; 5   6. 2 ; 6 ; 3 ; 2

30 Playing Badminton

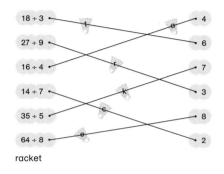

racket

31 Christmas Greetings

1. Anna   2. Jimmy   3. Amy
4. Jason   5. Jean

32 Completing Shapes

8 – C ; H   9 – A ; F

6 – B ; G   7 – D ; E

33 What a Birthday Gift!

1. 7   2. 40   3. 4
4. 28   5. 3   6. 9
7. 45   8. 15   9. 5
10. bicycle

34 Numbered Bears

A. 27   B. 3   C. 20
D. 9   E. 42   F. 4
G. 16   H. 8   I. 10
J. 5

35 Ready for a Race

1. B   2. F   3. E
4. C   5. G   6. A
7. D   8. H

36 Halloween Treats

1. 27 ; 5 ; 2 ; 5 ; 2   2. 19 ; 3 ; 4 ; 3 ; 4
3. 23 ; 4 ; 3 ; 4 ; 3

37   A Stony Way

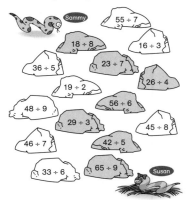

40   To the Forest

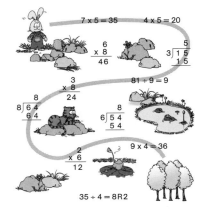

38   What Is the Shape?

1.	21	2.	32	3.	8
4.	9	5.	40	6.	6
7.	4	8.	15	9.	18
10.	63	11.	7	12.	2
13.	48	14.	27	15.	3
16.	5	17.	10	18.	56
19.	72	20.	20	21.	30
22.	36	23.	1	24.	42

25.

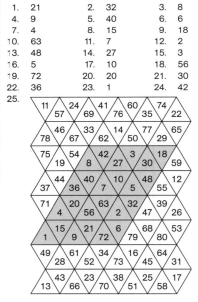

26.   parallelogram

39   Santa Claus Is Coming

(Individual drawing)

42	15	8	60	6	24	81	52	40	74	61	14	1	32
9	47	35	53	18	17	59	78	2	11	51	19	21	58
64	49	0	76	5	72	43	22	27	23	70	38	36	41
28	55	20	29	45	39	50	37	48	57	13	26	54	46
3	63	4	62	10	7	16	68	56	12	25	44	30	80

41   Two Good Friends

42   The Beautiful Fishes

1.	2 ; 10	2.	10 ; 2 ; 5 or 10 ; 5 ; 2
3.	3 ; 12	4.	12 ; 3 ; 4 or 12 ; 4 ; 3
5.	5 ; 15	6.	15 ; 5 ; 3 or 15 ; 3 ; 5
7.	4 ; 8	8.	8 ; 4 ; 2 or 8 ; 2 ; 4

Food for Betty

Granny Bear bought a lot of food for Betty Bear. Divide and colour the food with an answer of 6 to see what Granny bought.

$54 \div 9$

$36 \div 6$

$45 \div 5$

$18 \div 3$

$32 \div 4$

$42 \div 7$

$14 \div 2$

$48 \div 8$

What Are Their Names?

Draw lines to join the dogs to their houses. Find out their names.

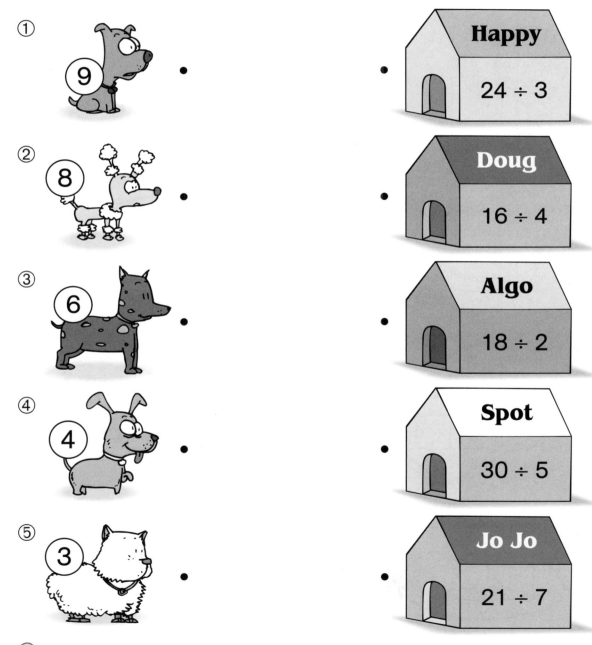

① 9

② 8

③ 6

④ 4

⑤ 3

Happy 24 ÷ 3

Doug 16 ÷ 4

Algo 18 ÷ 2

Spot 30 ÷ 5

Jo Jo 21 ÷ 7

The Carnival

Balloons of different colours are sold in the carnival. Divide and colour the balloons that have the same answers with the same colour.

$9\overline{)72}$

$4\overline{)20}$

$7\overline{)28}$

$8\overline{)56}$

$3\overline{)24}$

$2\overline{)14}$

$5\overline{)25}$

$6\overline{)30}$

$8\overline{)32}$

$6\overline{)48}$

$9\overline{)36}$

$7\overline{)35}$

Hens and Eggs

Divide and colour the eggs to match the hens.

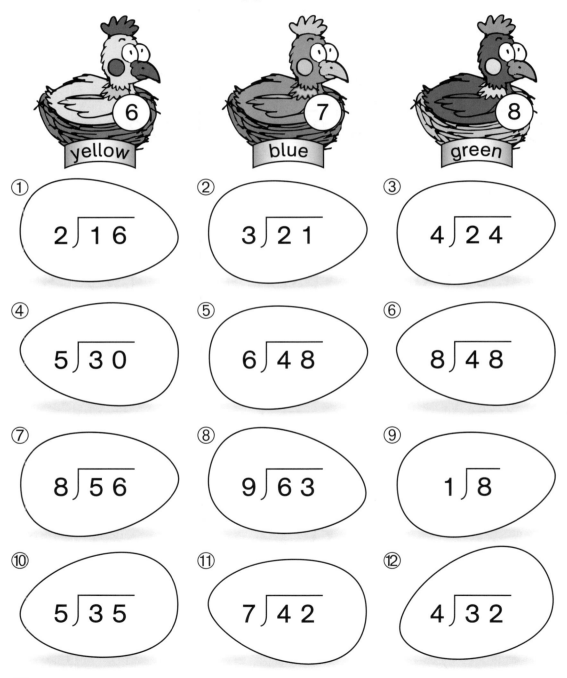

yellow   **6**

blue   **7**

green   **8**

① 2)1 6

② 3)2 1

③ 4)2 4

④ 5)3 0

⑤ 6)4 8

⑥ 8)4 8

⑦ 8)5 6

⑧ 9)6 3

⑨ 1)8

⑩ 5)3 5

⑪ 7)4 2

⑫ 4)3 2

A Visit to a Friend

Divide. Colour the path with the same quotient. Help Elaine get to Ted's house.

18 ÷ 3   12 ÷ 2   21 ÷ 3

42 ÷ 6   35 ÷ 5   24 ÷ 4   25 ÷ 5

10 ÷ 2   36 ÷ 6   6 ÷ 1   40 ÷ 8

35 ÷ 7   48 ÷ 8   45 ÷ 9   14 ÷ 2

20 ÷ 4   30 ÷ 5   42 ÷ 7

What's That?

Divide and write the letters to find out what it is.

① $18 \div 2 =$ _____ i

② $25 \div 5 =$ _____ e

③ $16 \div 8 =$ _____ g

④ $49 \div 7 =$ _____ l

⑤ $4 \div 1 =$ _____ o

⑥ $4 \div 4 =$ _____ r   ⑦ $48 \div 6 =$ _____ s

⑧ $9 \div 3 =$ _____ a   ⑨ $54 \div 9 =$ _____ l

⑩

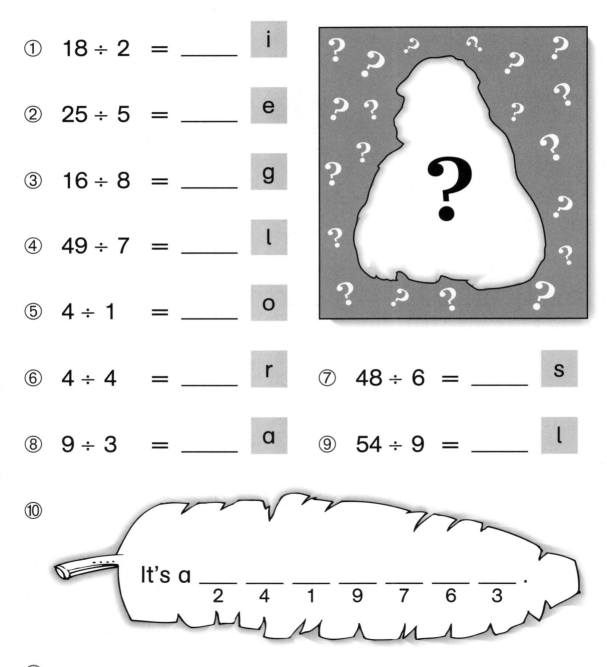

It's a ___ ___ ___ ___ ___ ___ ___ .
   2   4   1   9   7   6   3

Happy Birthday

Divide. Then write the representing letters for quotients in odd numbers in order from least to greatest. See how many candles Mom puts on Michelle's birthday cake.

① i $8\overline{)24}$

② x $5\overline{)20}$

③ n $3\overline{)18}$

④ s $9\overline{)72}$

⑤ e $7\overline{)7}$

⑥ h $4\overline{)28}$

⑦ g $6\overline{)30}$

⑧ t $2\overline{)18}$

⑨ v $7\overline{)56}$

⑩ Mom puts _____ candles on the birthday cake.

In the Circus

Divide the things for the clowns and animals.

① 3 clowns share 15 balloons.

Each clown has _____ balloons.

_____ ÷ _____ = _____

② 2 elephants share 4 umbrellas.

Each elephant has _____ umbrellas.

_____ ÷ _____ = _____

③ 6 seals share 12 balls.

Each seal has _____ balls.

_____ ÷ _____ = _____

④ 6 seals share 6 hats.

Each seal has _____ hat.

_____ ÷ _____ = _____

⑤ 2 elephants share 10 pennants.

Each elephant has _____ pennants.

_____ ÷ _____ = _____

⑥ 3 clowns share 6 rings.

Each clown has _____ rings.

_____ ÷ _____ = _____

 **30**

Playing Badminton

Draw lines to connect the division sentences to the answers. Use the letter on the same line with each answer to help solve the riddle.

18 ÷ 3 •   t   a   • 4

27 ÷ 9 •   • 6

16 ÷ 4 •   r   • 7

14 ÷ 7 •   k   • 3

35 ÷ 5 •   c   • 8

64 ÷ 8 •   e   • 2

What is a shuttlecock most afraid of ?

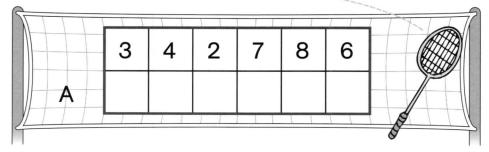

	3	4	2	7	8	6
A						

Christmas Greetings

Michelle is sending Christmas cards to her friends. Multiply or divide. Match the cards with the envelopes.

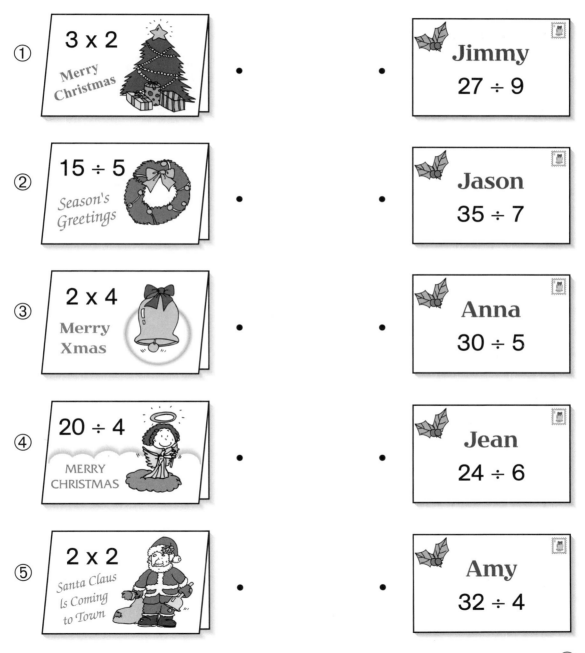

① 3 x 2
Merry Christmas

② 15 ÷ 5
Season's Greetings

③ 2 x 4
Merry Xmas

④ 20 ÷ 4
MERRY CHRISTMAS

⑤ 2 x 2
Santa Claus Is Coming to Town

Jimmy
27 ÷ 9

Jason
35 ÷ 7

Anna
30 ÷ 5

Jean
24 ÷ 6

Amy
32 ÷ 4

Multiply or divide. Match the answers and then colour each shape and its parts with the same colour to help Ted complete the 2-D shapes.

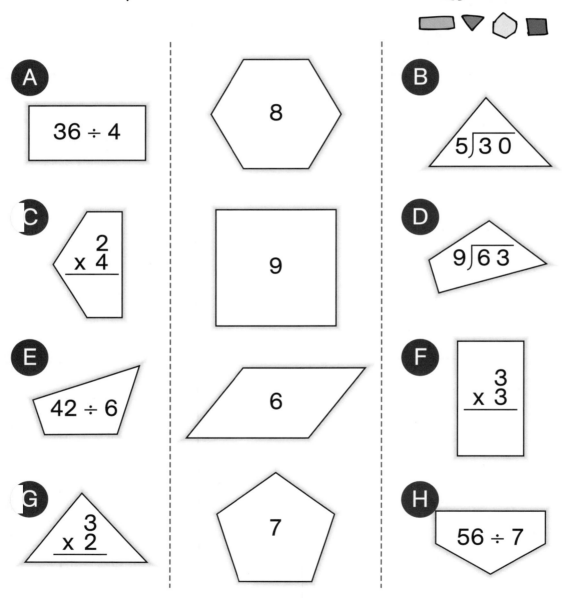

A $36 \div 4$

8

B $5\overline{)30}$

C $\begin{array}{r} 2 \\ \times\ 4 \end{array}$

9

D $9\overline{)63}$

E $42 \div 6$

6

F $\begin{array}{r} 3 \\ \times\ 3 \end{array}$

G $\begin{array}{r} 3 \\ \times\ 2 \end{array}$

7

H $56 \div 7$

Multiply or divide. Then write the letters to find out the gift that Michelle got for her birthday.

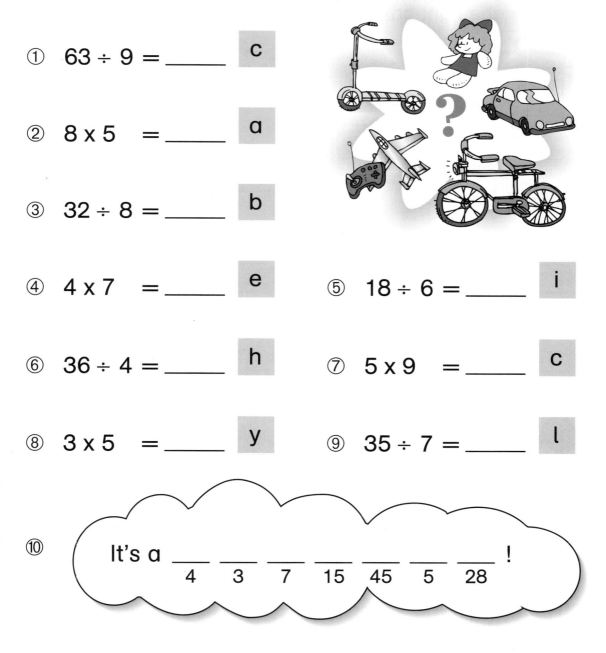

① 63 ÷ 9 = _____ c

② 8 x 5 = _____ a

③ 32 ÷ 8 = _____ b

④ 4 x 7 = _____ e

⑤ 18 ÷ 6 = _____ i

⑥ 36 ÷ 4 = _____ h

⑦ 5 x 9 = _____ c

⑧ 3 x 5 = _____ y

⑨ 35 ÷ 7 = _____ l

⑩ It's a __ __ __ __ __ __ __ !
        4   3   7   15   45   5   28

 **34** # Numbered Bears

The zoologists number the bears to keep track of their activities. Multiply or divide. Then write the numbers of the bears in the right boxes.

Bear A
$$3 \times 9$$

Bear B
$$6 \overline{)18}$$

Bear C
$$5 \times 4$$

Bear D
$$5 \overline{)45}$$

Bear E
$$6 \times 7$$

Bear F
$$7 \overline{)28}$$

Bear G
$$2 \times 8$$

Bear H
$$4 \overline{)32}$$

Bear I
$$5 \times 2$$

Bear J
$$8 \overline{)40}$$

Ready for a Race

Multiply or divide. Then match the number sentences with the answers to help the drivers find their racing cars.   Write the representing letters on their helmets.

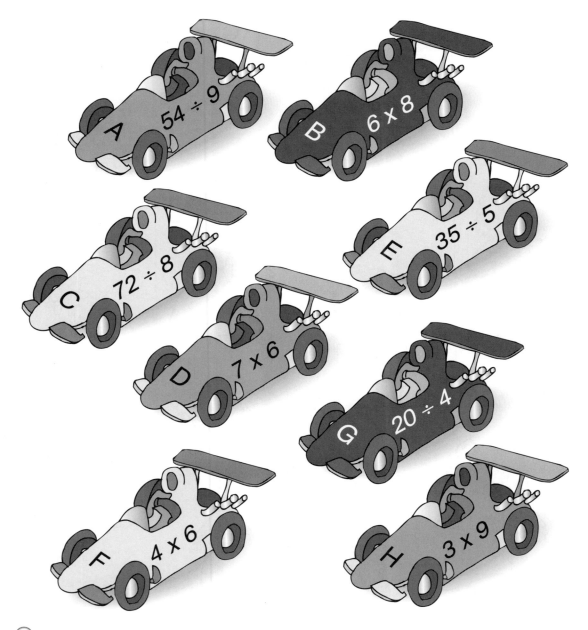

Halloween Treats

5 children are sharing the treats they have got. Complete the division sentence in each group and fill in the missing numbers.

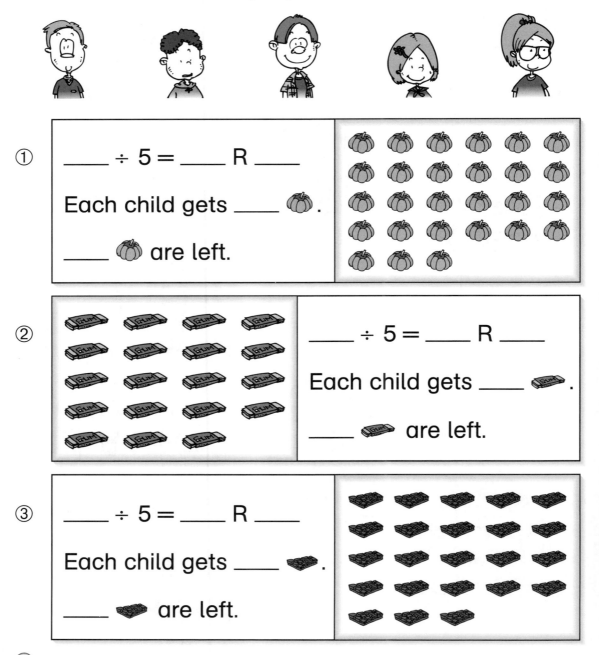

① _____ ÷ 5 = _____ R _____

Each child gets _____ 🎃.

_____ 🎃 are left.

② _____ ÷ 5 = _____ R _____

Each child gets _____ 🍬.

_____ 🍬 are left.

③ _____ ÷ 5 = _____ R _____

Each child gets _____ 🍫.

_____ 🍫 are left.

A Stony Way

Divide and colour the stones with a remainder of 2. Help Sammy Snake get to Susan Snake.

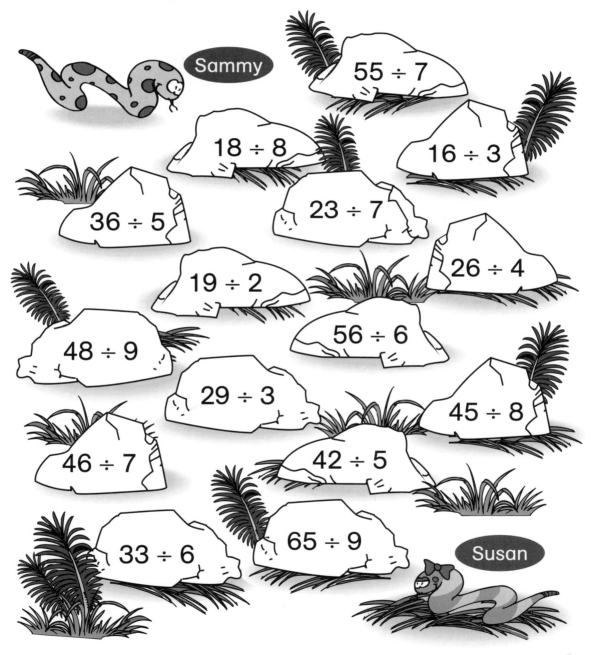

Sammy

$55 \div 7$

$18 \div 8$

$16 \div 3$

$36 \div 5$

$23 \div 7$

$26 \div 4$

$19 \div 2$

$48 \div 9$

$56 \div 6$

$29 \div 3$

$45 \div 8$

$46 \div 7$

$42 \div 5$

$33 \div 6$

$65 \div 9$

Susan

What Is the Shape?

Colour the triangles in ㉕ with the answers from the following number sentences. Then write the name of the coloured shape.

① 3 x 7 = _____

② 4 x 8 = _____

③ 72 ÷ 9 = _____

④ 54 ÷ 6 = _____

⑤ 5 x 8 = _____

⑥ 24 ÷ 4 = _____

⑦ 28 ÷ 7 = _____

⑧ 3 x 5 = _____

⑨ 2 x 9 = _____

⑩ 9 x 7 = _____

⑪ 14 ÷ 2 = _____

⑫ 10 ÷ 5 = _____

⑬ 6 x 8 = _____

⑭ 9 x 3 = _____

⑮ 24 ÷ 8 = _____

⑯ 35 ÷ 7 = _____

⑰ 5 x 2 = _____

⑱ 8 x 7 = _____

⑲ 9 x 8 = _____

⑳ 5 x 4 = _____

㉑ 6 x 5 = _____

㉒ 4 x 9 = _____

㉓ 1 ÷ 1 = _____

㉔ 7 x 6 = _____

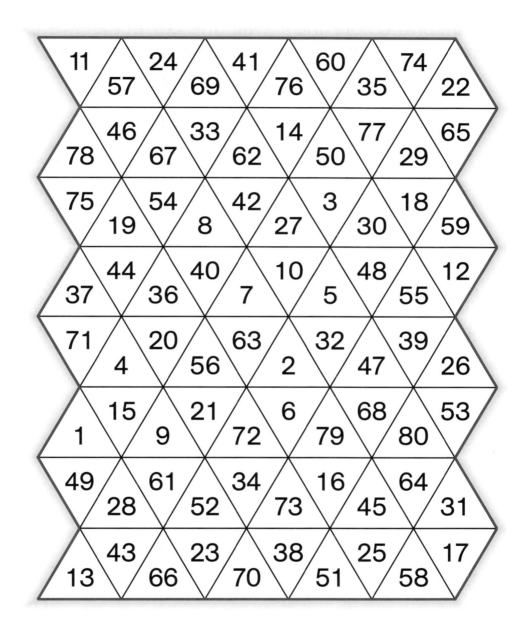

㉖ It is a _____ .

Santa Claus Is Coming

Calculate and colour the ☐ with the correct answers. The coloured numbers would reveal what to draw on Santa Claus.

8 x 8		54 ÷ 9
3 x 9		2 x 7
16 ÷ 4	9 x 8	8 x 2
5 x 6	7 x 6	8 x 4
5 x 5	56 ÷ 8	48 ÷ 6
9 x 5	8 x 7	9 x 4
5 x 8	21 ÷ 7	18 ÷ 9
8 x 3	9 x 9	7 x 7
6 x 8	4 x 7	27 ÷ 3
6 x 2	2 x 9	1 ÷ 1
7 x 3	5 x 2	45 ÷ 9
9 x 6	3 x 5	4 x 5
7 x 5	9 x 7	9 x 0

42	15	8	60	6	24	81	52	40	74	61	14	1	32
9	47	35	53	18	17	59	78	2	11	51	19	21	58
64	49	0	76	5	72	43	22	27	23	70	38	36	41
28	55	20	29	45	39	50	37	48	57	13	26	54	46
3	63	4	62	10	7	16	68	56	12	25	44	30	80

Multiply or divide. Help Benny Bunny go to the forest by
following the path with the correct answers.

$7 \times 5 = 35$ $4 \times 5 = 20$

$$\begin{array}{r} 6 \\ \times\ 8 \\ \hline 4\ 6 \end{array}$$

$$\begin{array}{r} 5 \\ 3\overline{)1\ 5} \\ 1\ 5 \\ \hline \end{array}$$

$$\begin{array}{r} 3 \\ \times\ 8 \\ \hline 2\ 4 \end{array}$$

$81 \div 9 = 9$

$$\begin{array}{r} 8 \\ 8\overline{)6\ 4} \\ 6\ 4 \\ \hline \end{array}$$

$$\begin{array}{r} 8 \\ 6\overline{)5\ 4} \\ 5\ 4 \\ \hline \end{array}$$

$9 \times 4 = 36$

$$\begin{array}{r} 2 \\ \times\ 6 \\ \hline 1\ 2 \end{array}$$

$35 \div 4 = 8R2$

Two Good Friends

Multiply or divide. Write the answers in the ☐. Help Freddie Frog get to Fion Frog.

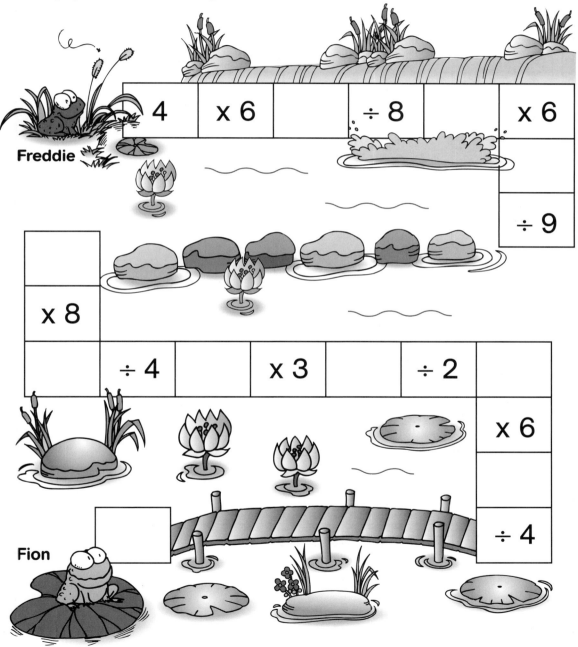

Freddie

4 | x 6 | | ÷ 8 | | x 6

÷ 9

x 8

÷ 4 | | x 3 | | ÷ 2

x 6

÷ 4

Fion

The Beautiful Fishes

Look at the different fishes in the aquariums. Complete a fact family for each group of fish.

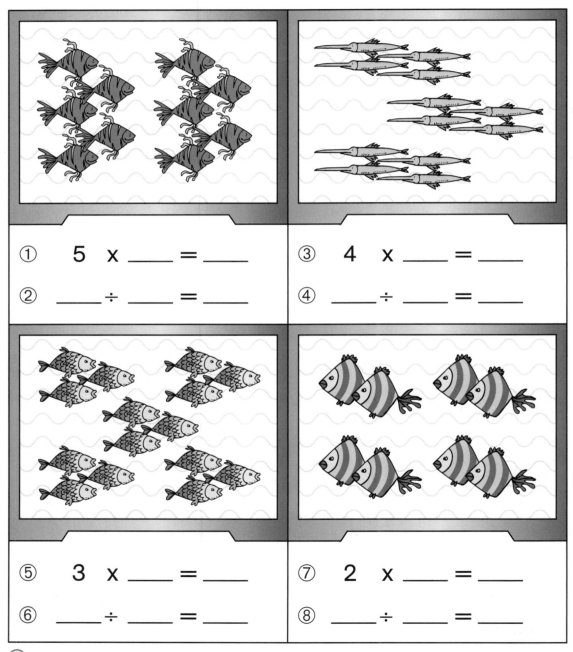

①   5   x ____ = ____

②   ____ ÷ ____ = ____

③   4   x ____ = ____

④   ____ ÷ ____ = ____

⑤   3   x ____ = ____

⑥   ____ ÷ ____ = ____

⑦   2   x ____ = ____

⑧   ____ ÷ ____ = ____